W9-AYQ-929

# The Yangstze

## China's Majestic River

### By Molly Aloian

CRABTREE
Publishing Company
www.crabtreebooks.com

# Crabtree Publishing Company

www.crabtreebooks.com

**Author**: Molly Aloian
**Editor**: Barbara Bakowski
**Designer**: Tammy West, Westgraphix LLC
**Photo Researcher**: Edward A. Thomas
**Map Illustrator**: Stefan Chabluk
**Indexer**: Nila Glikin
**Project Coordinator**: Kathy Middleton
**Crabtree Editor**: Adrianna Morganelli
**Production Coordinator**: Kenneth Wright
**Prepress Technician**: Kenneth Wright

**Series Consultant**: Michael E. Ritter, Ph.D., Professor
of Geography, University of Wisconsin—Stevens Point

Developed for Crabtree Publishing Company by RJF
Publishing LLC (www.RJFpublishing.com)

**Cover**: The Three Gorges Dam, the world's largest
hydroelectric dam, spans the Yangtze River near the
city of Yichang, China.

**Photo Credits**:
Cover: Xinhua/Landov
4: View Stock/Photolibrary
6: TAO Images Limited/Photolibrary
7: © Charles Ridgway/Alamy
8: Xinhua/Landov
10, 12: AP Images
13, 18, 27: iStockphoto
14: © Dennis Cox/Alamy
16: Emperor Chu Yuan-Chang
  (1328- 98), founder of the Ming Dynasty (pen, ink, and
  opaque watercolor on paper) by Chinese school/
  National Palace Museum, Taipei,
  Taiwan/The Bridgeman Art Library
20: DAJ/Getty Images
22: WEN ZHENXIAO/Xinhua/Landov
23: © Danita Delimont/Alamy
24: Getty Images
26: View Stock/Photolibrary

**Library and Archives Canada Cataloguing in Publication**

Aloian, Molly
  The Yangtze : China's majestic river / Molly Aloian.

(Rivers around the world)
Includes index.
ISBN 978-0-7787-7449-5 (bound).--ISBN 978-0-7787-7472-3 (pbk.)

    1. Yangtze River (China)--Juvenile literature. 2. Yangtze River
Valley
(China)--Juvenile literature. I. Title. II. Series: Rivers around the
world

DS793.Y3A46 2010       j951'.2       C2009-906241-0

5408

**Library of Congress Cataloging-in-Publication Data**

Aloian, Molly.
 The Yangtze : China's majestic river / by Molly Aloian
    p. cm. -- (Rivers around the world)
 Includes index.
 ISBN 978-0-7787-7472-3 (pbk. : alk. paper) -- ISBN 978-0-7787-7449-5
(reinforced library binding : alk. paper)
 1. Rivers--Juvenile literature. 2. River life--Juvenile literature. 3.
Stream ecology--Juvenile literature. I. Title. II. Series.

 GB1203.8.A56 2010
 951'.2--dc22

                                    2009042412

**Crabtree Publishing Company**
www.crabtreebooks.com    1-800-387-7650

Printed in the U.S.A./122009/BG20091103

**Published in Canada**
**Crabtree Publishing**
616 Welland Ave.
St. Catharines, ON
L2M 5V6

**Published in the United States**
**Crabtree Publishing**
PMB 59051
350 Fifth Avenue, 59th Floor
New York, New York 10118

**Published in the United
Kingdom**
**Crabtree Publishing**
Maritime House
Basin Road North, Hove
BN41 1WR

**Published in Australia**
**Crabtree Publishing**
386 Mt. Alexander Rd.
Ascot Vale (Melbourne)
VIC 3032

# CONTENTS

Words that are defined in the glossary are in **bold** type
the first time they appear in the text.

# CHAPTER 1

# River to Heaven

For thousands of years, the awe-inspiring Yangtze River has sustained life in China. Countless generations of Chinese people have relied on the river for fresh drinking water, crop **irrigation**, and fishing. **Barges** loaded with cargo have moved products throughout the river basin. Today, the rushing waters of the Yangtze River also help provide electricity to power the world's fastest-growing **economy**. But the river has brought death as well as life, killing thousands of people in devastating floods during its long history.

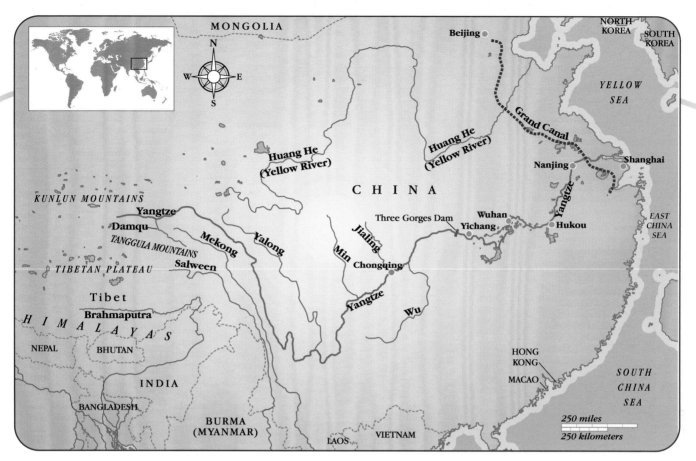

The Yangtze River is a major transportation route in China, connecting the interior with the coast.

The Yangtze River is the longest river in Asia. At 3,915 miles (6,300 kilometers) long, it is also the third-longest river in the world. From its source in the mountains of western China, the Yangtze River flows southeast and then east across south-central and east-central China. It empties into the East China Sea near the city of Shanghai. The Yangtze River is China's most important navigable waterway. It also acts as a natural boundary—both geographic and cultural—between the northern and southern parts of the country.

**FAST FACT**
In 2008, the population of China was more than 1.3 billion. About 400 million people—nearly one-third of the country's population—live in the Yangtze River basin.

LEFT: The Yantze River winds through spectacular landscapes, including the Three Gorges area, long known as a culturally and historically important site and now as the location of the Three Gorges Dam.

After descending from the Tanggula Mountains in the northern Tibetan Plateau, the Yangtze River makes a dramatic turn near the small town of Shigu in southwestern China.

## Economic Importance

The Yangtze River plays an important role in China's economy. The river provides irrigation water for agriculture, a source of **hydroelectricity**, a waterway for boats carrying huge amounts of cargo, and sites of interest for tourists. It is a key transportation route through some of the most densely populated and economically important areas in China. The land that makes up the Yangtze **drainage basin** contributes almost half of the total agricultural output of China.

Some of China's most important industrial centers are located on the Yangtze River, including the cities of Wuhan and Chongqing. Many dams have been constructed on the Yangtze River and its **tributaries**. In 1994, construction began on the Three Gorges Dam, which is the world's largest hydroelectric dam. The dam enables large oceangoing

## Long River

People in China have many names for the Yangtze River. It is called Chang Jiang, which means "Long River," and Da Jiang, which means "Great River." High in the mountains of Tibet, people call the river Tongtian He, which means "River to Heaven." Upstream from the ancient city of Yibin, people call it Jinsha Jiang, or "Golden Sand River." Outside China, it has sometimes been called the Blue River, to differentiate it from the Huang He, or Yellow River.

Ancient plowing methods are still in use at this rice farm along the Yangtze River in central China.

cargo ships to navigate 1,400 miles (2,250 km) inland from the East China Sea to Chongqing.

## Variety of Life

The Yangtze River flows through a variety of **ecosystems**, including mountains, valleys, forests, and **wetlands**. Many rare and endangered animal and plant species live in the river basin. One of Earth's most threatened animals, the giant panda, lives in the forested mountainous areas of southwest China. The rare Chinese alligator inhabits the Yangtze River. Yangtze River dolphins once lived there, too, but many scientists believe that these animals are now **extinct**.

## A Center of Civilization

The Yangtze basin is one of the longest-inhabited regions in China and the site of important ancient civilizations. Thousands of years ago, people traveled and transported goods on the river, fished in its waters, and hunted for animals along its banks. They also used the water to irrigate crops, such as rice and wheat. The river enabled the people of China to develop one of the most advanced civilizations in the ancient world.

## Under Threat

Many people are worried that human activities are a serious threat to the Yangtze's ecosystems—and perhaps to global weather and climate. Large-scale logging and agriculture have contributed to **deforestation** and pollution. Increases in population and industry also threaten the health of the river. The biggest threat, however, is the Three Gorges Dam. Changing the flow of water has had damaging environmental effects, including the destruction of animal **habitats**.

# CHAPTER 2

# The Mighty Yangtze

The Yangtze River and its basin started to form approximately 40 million years ago. Many people think of the river as having three sections, each of which includes different ecosystems. The upper Yangtze stretches from the river's source in Qinghai province to the city of Yichang in Hubei province. A province is a political division of the country. The middle Yangtze flows from Yichang to Hukou, in Jiangxi province. The lower Yangtze flows from Hukou to the East China Sea.

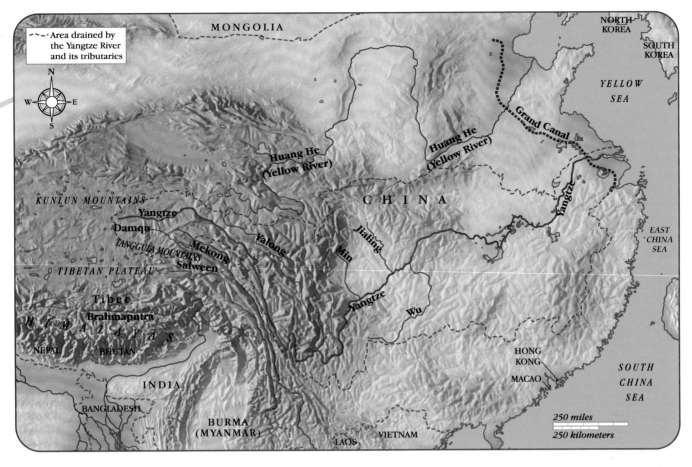

The Yangtze River drains almost one-fifth of China's total land area.

## Geologic History

About 40 million years ago, drifting Indian and **Eurasian** landmasses collided, causing huge areas of land to be pushed upward. The jagged peaks of the Himalayas and the Tibetan Plateau were formed. A **plateau** is a broad, flat area of high land. The collision also produced China's general **drainage pattern**, in which all the major rivers flow from west to east.

A drainage pattern refers to the arrangement of a main stream and its tributaries. The Yangtze River has a **dendritic** drainage pattern.

This pattern typically occurs in level areas made up of a single type of rock. A dendritic drainage pattern looks like the branches of a tree. The Yangtze River drains, or carries away the surface water from, about 690,000 square miles (1.8 million square km) of land.

## Upper Course

In 2009, Chinese scientists said they had determined the source of the Yangtze River to be the Damqu River. These waters come from a **glacier** on the slopes of the Tanggula Mountains

LEFT: Melting ice from glaciers like this one in the Tanggula Mountains feeds the Damqu River, the source of the Yangtze River.

A small boat travels on the Yangtze River in the Wu Xia Gorge, the middle gorge of the famous Three Gorges, before the water level rose following construction of the Three Gorges Dam.

## Three Gorges Dam

Construction of the Three Gorges Dam began in 1994, and the main work was completed by 2008. The dam is more than 600 feet (180 meters) high and about 1.5 miles (2.4 km) wide. The dam was designed to prevent floods downstream, to provide an important source of electricity to meet growing demands, and to improve navigation on the Yangtze River. However, the dam would have to create a **reservoir** that would flood hundreds of towns and villages in Hubei and Sichuan provinces. As a result, 1.3 million people had to be relocated before the dam was finished.

of Tibet. The river begins its course flowing east through a shallow valley. It winds its way south down snow-covered mountain peaks that are cut with **gorges**.

For several hundred miles, the Yangtze flows southeast, then it turns northeast. In this part of its course, the river flows in rushing rapids. It receives water from many tributaries, including the Yalong, Min, Jialing, and Wu rivers. Beyond Chongqing, the river continues northeast and then drops through the Three Gorges—Qutang Xia, Wu Xia, and Xiling Xia.

The Three Gorges Dam is near the city of Yichang.

## Middle Course

In the middle of its course, the Yangtze River flows through a large plain with many lakes. Before construction of the Three Gorges Dam, this part of the river was prone to severe flooding. The floods deposited large amounts of nutrient-rich material called **silt** on the land alongside the riverbanks. Silt makes soil fertile, or good for growing crops.

## Lower Course

From the city of Hukou, the Yangtze River makes a gentle descent through plains, hills, and a coastal wetland with several shallow lakes. The river then passes a number of large cities, entering the sea near Shanghai. Near its **mouth**, the Yangtze River stretches about nine miles (14 km) across. Its **delta** is made up of a large number of tributaries, lakes, and marshes.

## Destructive Floods

Between March and August, there are heavy **monsoon** rains in the Yangtze River's lower and middle courses. Heavy rains fall in the upper course from May to September. In the past, floods were common throughout the Yangtze basin. Floods washed away homes, farms, and businesses. In 1931,

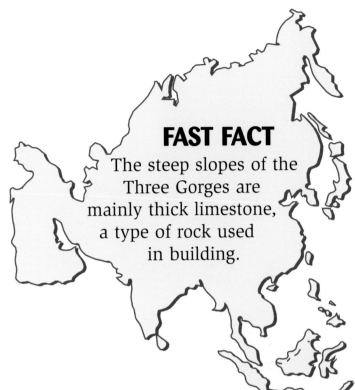

**FAST FACT**
The steep slopes of the Three Gorges are mainly thick limestone, a type of rock used in building.

Yangtze River floods killed 145,000 people. In 1935, more than 142,000 people died. A recent major flood, in 1998, killed more than 3,000 people and left millions homeless.

## Plant Life

Thousands of species of plants live along the banks of the Yangtze River. The golden arch, a rare species of tree, grows in the Yangtze River valley. Its coin-shaped leaves are green in spring and summer and turn yellow in autumn. Bamboo, magnolia, and gingko trees also grow within the basin. A number of different types of algae live in the river, providing food for many species of fish.

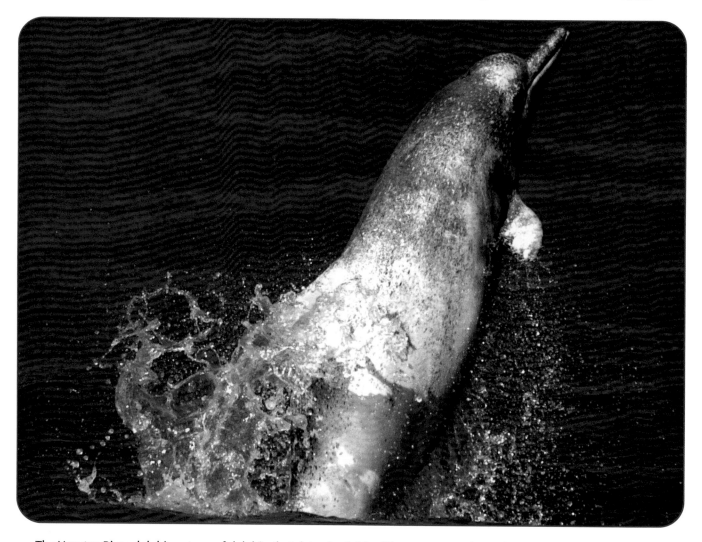

The Yangtze River dolphin, a type of dolphin that dates back 20 million years, may have died out completely in 2006, according to scientists.

People grow food crops in the rich soil of the river basin. Major crops include rice, wheat, corn, barley, sweet potatoes, and legumes.

## Animals Abound

Salamanders, soft-shell turtles, frogs, birds, and other animals live near the river. Otters swim in the water, hunting for fish. Hundreds of species of fish, including carp, catfish, Chinese sturgeon, and Chinese paddlefish, swim in the Yangtze River and its tributaries. Sturgeon can grow to be 16 feet (five m) long. The central Yangtze River is an important habitat for **migratory** birds, including almost the entire wintering Siberian white crane population.

A symbol of strength and perseverance in China, the Chinese alligator has become rare in the Yangtze River. Scientists breed the alligators in captivity to help prevent the species from becoming extinct.

The Yangtze River dolphin, however, is believed to have become extinct in 2006. In the late 1980s, the population of river dolphins was about 400, but by the mid-1990s the number had dropped to fewer than 100. Scientists say overfishing, which leaves the dolphins without a food source, as well as dams, ship traffic, and pollution are to blame. Dams affected the river dolphins' habitat and interrupted their movements upstream.

Scientists are working to save the Yangtze River finless porpoise from the same fate. Fewer than 400 finless porpoises may remain in the river.

**FAST FACT**

People in China called the Yangtze River dolphin "the goddess of the Yangtze."

## Lovely Lotus

Lotus plants grow on mud flats in the eastern part of the Yangtze River valley. The plant's disk-shaped leaves can be almost three feet (0.9 m) wide! They usually float on the surface of the water. The flowers are pink or white. People eat the plant's roots and use them to make tea. In China, the lotus plant symbolizes purity. Lotus plants and flowers have been featured in Chinese art and literature for centuries.

# CHAPTER 3

# Flowing Through History

Thousands of years ago, Chinese civilizations developed in the Yangtze basin because the river was a source of life. The river provided water for drinking and for growing food crops. Flooding deposited nutrients that left the soil rich for farming. Cities developed in the fertile Yangtze basin, as an economy based on agriculture developed.

This map shows the extent of land controlled by various dynasties during different periods of China's ancient history.

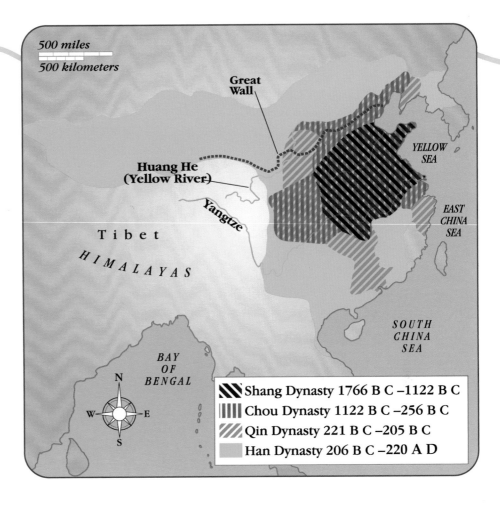

500 miles
500 kilometers

Great Wall

Huang He (Yellow River)

Yangtze

Tibet

HIMALAYAS

YELLOW SEA

EAST CHINA SEA

SOUTH CHINA SEA

BAY OF BENGAL

N W E S

▨ Shang Dynasty 1766 B C –1122 B C
▥ Chou Dynasty 1122 B C –256 B C
▧ Qin Dynasty 221 B C –205 B C
▨ Han Dynasty 206 B C –220 A D

## Early Settlements

The earliest known settlements in China were farming villages along the banks of the Yangtze River and China's other major river, the Huang He (Yellow River). Over time, agricultural success helped village populations grow, and the villages grew into states, or organized political territories. The rulers of the strongest states were able to expand the territories over which they ruled. Control of the kingdoms passed from generation to generation in powerful ruling families, known as dynasties. Periods of China's ancient history are named after the dynasties.

## Dynamic Dynasties

The Shang dynasty began in about 1766 BC and lasted until about 1122 BC. The Chou dynasty (1122 BC to 256 BC) followed, changing the way China was governed. Chou rulers permitted warriors to own land if they promised to fight for their ruler in war.

The Qin dynasty began in 221 BC, when Qin Shihuangdi came to power. He was China's first emperor and controlled a much larger area than the previous dynasties. He began building the Great Wall, to protect China from invaders.

During the Han dynasty (206 BC to 220 AD), about two-thirds of China's

LEFT: The city of Suzhou lies along the Grand Canal, built during the Sui dynasty (581 AD to 618 AD), to connect the Huang He and the Yangtze River.

## Irrigation System

In 256 BC, the governor of Sichuan province in southwest China set up an irrigation system to control the flooding of the Min River, a tributary of the upper Yangtze. The Dujiangyan Irrigation System splits the river into an inner flow for irrigation and an outer channel for flood control. The irrigation system, which is still in use today, made the land of the Chengdu plains some of the most fertile farmland in China. The Dujiangyan Irrigation System is the oldest and only surviving no-dam irrigation system in the world. In 2000, it was added to the World Heritage List as a cultural site.

people were small-scale farmers. They grew crops such as rice, beans, gourds, snow peas, strawberries, dates, and melons. The Yangtze River and its tributaries provided irrigation water.

## Tang and Song Dynasties

The Tang dynasty, which began in 618 AD, is often referred to as China's "golden age." The army was strong, and it was an era of great artistic achievements. During this time, China became one of the wealthiest and most powerful regions in the world. In 906 AD, the Tang dynasty collapsed.

Later dynasties, including the Song dynasty (960 AD–1279 AD), brought an increase in trade. Chinese merchants got wealthy trading tea, silk, porcelain, jewelry, rice, other grains, and spices.

## Mongol Rule

In 1206 AD, the Mongols, from a region north of China, became unified under the leader Genghis Khan. In the years that followed, Mongol armies conquered and seized parts of China. By 1260 AD, the Mongol ruler Kublai Khan had captured northern China and become the emperor. By 1279 AD, he had conquered southern China and founded the Yuan dynasty. The Yuan dynasty ruled for about 90 years until a former **Buddhist** monk and military leader, Zhu Yuanzhang, took the throne as the first ruler of the Ming dynasty.

Emperor Zhu Yuanzhang (1328 AD-1398 AD) founded the Ming Dynasty.

## The Grand Canal

During the Sui dynasty (581 AD to 618 AD), emperors ordered the construction of a **canal** crossing the Huang He and the Yangtze rivers, to connect northern and southern China. People used the canal, known as the Grand Canal, to transport agricultural products from the Yangtze basin to northern China. The Sui emperors forced about six million laborers to work at building the canal. About 1,100 miles (1,770 km) long, it remains the world's longest human-made waterway. The canal flows through some of China's most historically important cities.

Originally built to transport grain from the south to Beijing, the Grand Canal today is an important shipping route for barges carrying goods such as bricks, gravel, sand, and coal.

## From Dynasty to Republic

The Ming dynasty brought a return to Chinese rule, during which arts and literature flourished. China also experienced growth in agriculture and trade. One important new farming practice was **crop rotation**, which kept fields continuously cultivated while maintaining the soil's fertility. The production of porcelain goods increased, especially the white porcelain with blue painting that is identified with the dynasty. Trade with foreign countries expanded.

In 1644, the Manchu attacked the Ming capital and began the Qing

NOTABLE QUOTE

*"Agriculture is the foundation of the empire. As for gold, pearls, and jade, they cannot be eaten in time of hunger, and cannot be worn in time of cold."*

—imperial decree from 141 BC

dynasty, the last Chinese dynasty ruled by an emperor. The Manchu were people who lived for many centuries mainly in a region of China historically known as Manchuria (now the Northeast). The Manchu ruled for more than 250 years. During the Qing dynasty, the territory of the empire grew to three times its size during the Ming dynasty.

## FAST FACT

Between the 7th and 14th centuries, China had the world's most advanced civilization. Important inventions, including paper, gunpowder, porcelain, silk, and the compass, originated in China and were later introduced to other parts of the world.

## Marco Polo in China

In 1275, the Italian explorer Marco Polo carried word of China's advanced civilization back to Europe. He wrote a book, called *The Travels of Marco Polo*, that was popular in his own time and for centuries afterward.

From *The Travels of Marco Polo*: "You must know that for three months of the year, December, January, and February, the Great Khan resides in the capital city of [China].... In that city stands his great palace.... The hall of the palace is so large that it could easily dine 6,000 people; and it is quite a marvel to see how many rooms there are besides. The building is altogether so vast, so rich, and so beautiful, that no man on Earth could design anything superior to it."

The population grew from about 150 million people to 450 million.

In 1911, people who wanted to bring about political change in China led a successful revolt against the Qing dynasty. In 1912, the Republic of China was established. A republic is a government that is not headed by a king or an emperor.

## Battles on the River

Throughout history, many important battles took place along the Yangtze River. In 208 AD, the Battle of Red Cliffs was fought along the south bank of the river. The battle occurred during a time of civil war around the end of the Han dynasty. Many centuries later, the largest uprising in modern Chinese history—the Taiping Rebellion—took place. From 1850 to 1864, battles raged along the Yangtze River as rebels attempted to overthrow the Qing dynasty.

During China's civil war of the 1930s and 1940s, **Communist** forces under leader Mao Zedong made several strategic crossings of the river and its tributaries. The Communists drove the Kuomintang (Chinese Nationalist) government from mainland China and formed the People's Republic of China in 1949.

## Modern People

The central part of China depends largely on the agricultural region drained by the Yangtze River. Some people live in bustling cities along the river and its tributaries and work in a wide variety of professions and industries. There are also remote villages along the river, especially in the highlands of the upper basin.

## City Profile: Shanghai

Shanghai, located near the mouth of the Yangtze River, is the most heavily populated city in China. It is the largest industrial and commercial center in China and is mainland China's most significant port. More than 18 million people live in Shanghai.

The Oriental Pearl Tower is a prominent feature of the city skyline of Shanghai.

# CHAPTER 4

# Travel and Commerce

For thousands of years, the Yangtze River has been an extremely important waterway for people and goods moving between Sichuan province in western China and the eastern coast of China. Today, it remains the region's main transportation route and is vital to commerce and industry in the Yangtze basin.

## Traveling by Boat

People have been traveling by boat on the Yangtze River since ancient times. People of the Han dynasty developed sailboats called junks. The sturdy, flat-bottomed junks were made of soft wood and had rudders for steering. People used these oceangoing boats to carry large amounts of cargo throughout the river basin.

Long ago, people also used smaller, flat-bottomed boats called sampans for river travel. Sampans were usually 12 to 15 feet (3.5 to 4.5 m) long and were propelled with short oars. Today, oceangoing vessels and large cargo and passenger ships can travel up the Yangtze River for more than 1,400 miles (2,250 km).

**FAST FACT**

Although only one-fourth of the Yangtze basin is suitable for farming, the basin contributes almost half of China's crop production.

## Land of Plenty

Much of the Yangtze basin's economy centers on agriculture. The soil and climate in Sichuan province, often called "the land of plenty" by its people, are ideal for growing rice, cotton, wheat, barley, corn, and beans. Farming also takes place in the lower basin and delta, as well as in the plains between the Yangtze River and its

tributary the Han. In some areas, two or three crops are harvested each year.

## Fishing and Fisheries

For many people living in the Yangtze basin, fishing is a major source of revenue. Hundreds of species of fish, including carp, bream, Chinese perch, and Chinese sturgeon, live in the Yangtze River and its tributaries. White and black amur are the most economically valuable species of fish.

LEFT: A traditional Chinese boat on the Yangtze River.

Economic development, however, has taken a toll on the river's fish populations. Since 2002, fishing has been banned during certain months along different stretches of the Yangtze River. The annual fishing ban is meant to help replenish and preserve fish species endangered by overfishing.

In 2009, 120,000 Chinese sturgeons were released into the Yangtze River in an effort to boost the population of the endangered species in the wild. The Chinese sturgeon is sometimes called a "living fossil." It is one of the world's oldest vertebrates, dating back about 140 million years. Fewer than 300 wild sturgeons were thought to be living in the Yangtze River prior to the 2009 release. The endangered fish's decline has been largely caused by pollution and illegal fishing.

The Three Gorges Dam on the Yangtze River is the largest hydroelectric project in the world.

## Irrigation and Electricity

Both the Three Gorges Dam and the Gezhou Dam are on the Yangtze River. The Gezhou Dam was completed in the 1980s and is located near Yichang, about 25 miles (40 km) downstream of the Three Gorges Dam site. These and other dams and canals supply the

NOTABLE QUOTE

*"Agriculture is the basic occupation of the world. So the imperial government must cut canals and ditches, guide the rivers, and build reservoirs in order to prevent flood and drought."*

—Wu Di, Han emperor, 111 BC

Shibaozhai ("Stone Treasure Fortress") is an ancient pagoda built against a cliff overlooking the Yangtze River. A wall was put in place to protect the pagoda when water levels rose following construction of the Three Gorges Dam.

region with irrigation water and electricity. The Three Gorges Dam generates more electricity than any other hydroelectric dam in the world. About 50 million tons of coal would need to be burned to produce the same amount of electricity annually. The dam also helps control flooding.

However, the Three Gorges Dam has created a new reservoir that has flooded many towns and cities along the Yangtze River. As a result, about 1.3 million people have been displaced. The reservoir created by the damming of the river extends 370 miles (600 km) upriver, to Chongqing.

## Industry Along the Yangtze

The Yangtze basin contains deposits of mineral resources, including coal, iron, and copper. Natural gas and oil are found in Sichuan province. Shanghai and Nanjing produce textiles, ships, iron and steel, and fertilizers. Industrialized areas around Chongqing and Chengdu produce cement, fertilizers, and iron and steel products.

## Tourism

Historical sites, such as the Shibaozhai Temple and the many **pagodas** along the Yangtze River, attract large numbers of Chinese visitors and foreign tourists each year. The Shibaozhai Temple was built on the northern bank of the river in the 1700s. Tourists visit Shanghai to see places such as the Bund, City God Temple, and the Oriental Pearl Tower. They also take guided boat tours through the Three Gorges.

# CHAPTER 5

# The River Today

Today, the Yangtze River provides for the water needs of one-third of China's population. Modern irrigation systems supply billions of gallons of water so that farmers can grow food and other crops year-round. The river provides people with fish to eat and water to drink. The Yangtze's Three Gorges Dam also provides hydroelectricity to the people of central and eastern China. But increased economic development and a growing population threaten the future of the river and the land around it.

## Deforestation in the Basin

One of the most serious problems in China is the destruction of forests. Land is cleared for agriculture, which wipes out the habitats of thousands of plant and animal species that live in the Yangtze River basin. Deforestation also contributes to flooding and erosion, or the gradual wearing away of soil by wind and water. Flooding occurs because clearing forests dramatically increases the surface **runoff** from rainfall. Without tree roots to anchor soil, the soil washes away into rivers and streams. Some experts say that as much as 40 percent of the Yangtze basin area has soil erosion problems.

**FAST FACT**
More than 85 percent of the original forests covering the Yangtze River basin have been cut down.

## Water and Air Pollution

The Yangtze River is polluted with untreated sewage and industrial waste. Chemicals used to kill pests on farmland enter the river in surface-water runoff.

Air pollution in the river basin is also a serious problem. Coal is burned to produce about three-quarters of China's electricity. But the process of burning coal releases carbon dioxide and other gases into the air. These gases build up in Earth's atmosphere and trap more of the Sun's heat close to Earth's surface. The trapped heat speeds up the rate of climate change. Other gases released during the burning of coal combine with moisture in the atmosphere, forming acid rain. When acid rain falls to Earth, it harms crops, forests, and waterways.

LEFT: People cross polluted water from the Yangtze River in Chongqing. The river is threatened by pollution from many sources, including discharge from about 10,000 chemical factories along its banks.

## Impact of the Three Gorges Dam

Harnessing the force of the Yangtze River to create hydroelectricity is a clean solution to China's increasing power demands. However, many scientists and other observers say that the environmental effects of the Three Gorges Dam are serious. Hundreds of factories, mines, and waste dumps were covered with water when the reservoir was created. Those submerged sites, along with huge industrial centers upstream, are creating pollution problems in the reservoir. Erosion of the steep hills around the reservoir is

Areas of grassland in China are becoming desert. Overgrazing by livestock strips the land of vegetation, and winds blow away the topsoil.

causing **landslides**. Erosion of downstream riverbanks threatens one of the world's biggest fisheries in the East China Sea.

## The Silt Situation

Before huge dams were built along the Yangtze River, the river carried hundreds of millions of tons of silt in the flow of its water. When the river flooded, silt nourished the lands along the riverbanks, making them fertile and productive. Where the river is dammed, silt collects at the bottom of reservoirs. This process is called siltation. The silt no longer reaches the Yangtze River's **floodplain**.

## Too Much Grazing

Overgrazing is another problem in the Yangtze River basin. Overgrazing occurs when too many livestock animals graze for food for extended periods of time. The animals destroy pastures bit by bit and ultimately cause permanent damage to the land. Overgrazing reduces the agricultural productivity of the land and is one cause of desertification. Desertification is the process of land becoming desert from poor land management practices, climate change, or a combination of both.

## Protecting the Yangtze

Scientists, engineers, politicians, environmentalists, and others are working to solve some of the Yangtze River's most serious problems. For example, International Rivers is an environmental organization that works to protect rivers and defend the communities that depend on rivers. The organization is monitoring the social and environmental effects of the Three Gorges Dam.

The World Wild Fund for Nature (WWF) in China works with local governments and businesses to protect the Yangtze River and its endangered species. Another WWF conservation program targets the forests and wildlife of the Minshan mountain range in Sichuan and Gansu provinces. Giant pandas, clouded leopards, golden monkeys, and pheasants live in this habitat.

The U.S.-based Nature Conservancy is working with the Chinese government, hydropower companies, and other organizations to minimize the environmental impact of the Three Gorges Dam and other dams planned for the Yangtze River. The Nature Conservancy is also working to restore the Yangtze River's wetlands, which play an important role in providing clean water to tens of millions of people. Many wetlands in the river basin have been drained for agriculture.

The endangered giant panda faces many threats, including destruction of its forest habitat.

NOTABLE QUOTE

*"We absolutely cannot relax our guard against ecological and environmental security problems sparked by the Three Gorges project. We cannot win passing economic prosperity at the cost of the environment."*

—Wang Xiaofeng, administrative director of the Three Gorges Dam, in 2007

# COMPARING THE WORLD'S RIVERS

| River | Continent | Source | Outflow | Approximate Length in miles (kilometers) | Area of Drainage Basin in square miles (square kilometers) |
|---|---|---|---|---|---|
| Amazon | South America | Andes Mountains, Peru | Atlantic Ocean | 4,000 (6,450) | 2.7 million (7 million) |
| Euphrates | Asia | Murat and Kara Su rivers, Turkey | Persian Gulf | 1,740 (2,800) | 171,430 (444,000) |
| Ganges | Asia | Himalayas, India | Bay of Bengal | 1,560 (2,510) | 400,000 (1 million) |
| Mississippi | North America | Lake Itasca, Minnesota | Gulf of Mexico | 2,350 (3,780) | 1.2 million (3.1 million) |
| Nile | Africa | Streams flowing into Lake Victoria, East Africa | Mediterranean Sea | 4,145 (6,670) | 1.3 million (3.3 million) |
| Rhine | Europe | Alps, Switzerland | North Sea | 865 (1,390) | 65,600 (170,000) |
| St. Lawrence | North America | Lake Ontario, Canada and United States | Gulf of St. Lawrence | 744 (1,190) | 502,000 (1.3 million) |
| Tigris | Asia | Lake Hazar, Taurus Mountains, Turkey | Persian Gulf | 1,180 (1,900) | 43,000 (111,000) |
| Yangtze | Asia | Damqu River, Tanggula Mountains, China | East China Sea | 3,915 (6,300) | 690,000 (1.8 million) |

# TIMELINE

| | |
|---|---|
| **About 5000 BC** | The first settlements develop along the Yangtze River. |
| **About 1766 BC** | The Shang dynasty begins. |
| **1122 BC** | The Chou dynasty begins. |
| **256 BC** | The Dujiangyan Irrigation System is begun to control the flooding of the Min River. |
| **221 BC** | China's first emperor unites much of present-day China; the Qin dynasty begins. |
| **206 BC** | The Han dynasty begins. |
| **581 AD — 618 AD** | The Grand Canal is built. |
| **618** | The Tang dynasty begins. |
| **960** | The Song dynasty begins. |
| **1206** | The Mongols unite under leader Genghis Khan. |
| **1275** | Marco Polo visits China. |
| **1279** | Mongol ruler Kublai Khan founds the Yuan dynasty. |
| **1368** | The Ming dynasty begins. |
| **1644** | The Qing dynasty begins. |
| **1912** | The Qing emperor steps down, and the Republic of China is established. |
| **1931** | Yangtze floods kill 145,000 people. |
| **1935** | More than 142,000 people die in Yangtze floods. |
| **1949** | Communists, led by Mao Zedong, win a civil war and take power in China. |
| **1950s** | Economic development increases in the Yangtze basin. |
| **1994** | Construction of the Three Gorges Dam begins. |
| **2006** | The Yangtze River dolphin is declared extinct. |
| **2008** | The Three Gorges Dam is completed. |

# GLOSSARY

**barges** Long, flat-bottomed boats used mostly for the transport of goods and usually propelled by towing

**Buddhist** A follower of the religion based on the teachings of Siddhartha Gautama, known as the Buddha (563 BC–483 BC)

**canal** A human-made waterway that is used for navigation and irrigation

**Communist** A person who believes that property and goods should be owned in common and labor should benefit all people

**crop rotation** The successive planting of different crops on the same land to improve soil fertility

**deforestation** The action or process of clearing an area of trees and underbrush

**delta** A triangular or fan-shaped area of land at the mouth of a river

**dendritic** Branching like a tree

**drainage basin** The land drained by a river and its tributaries

**drainage pattern** The arrangement of a main stream and its tributaries

**economy** The way money and goods are produced, distributed, and consumed

**ecosystems** Complex communities of organisms and their environments functioning as a unit

**Eurasian** Relating to a single landmass made up of Asia and Europe

**extinct** Having died out completely

**floodplain** The flat or nearly flat land along a river or stream or land that is covered by water during a flood

**glacier** A large body of ice and snow moving slowly down a slope or spreading outward on land

**gorges** Narrow canyons with steep walls

**habitat** The environment in which a plant or an animal naturally lives and grows

**hydroelectricity** Electricity that is produced by the force of moving water

**irrigation** The watering of land in an artificial way to foster plant growth

**landslides** Masses of rocks or earth that slip down a steep slope

**migratory** Moving periodically from one region to another for feeding or breeding

**monsoon** The season that is characterized by very heavy rainfall

**mouth** The place where a river enters a larger body of water

**pagoda** A tower in eastern Asia, usually with roofs curving upward at the division of each of several stories; it is erected as a temple

**plateau** A broad, flat area of high land

**reservoir** An artificial lake where water is collected and kept for use

**runoff** Water from rain or snow that flows over the surface of the ground and into rivers

**silt** Small particles of sand or rock left as sediment

**tributaries** Smaller rivers and streams that flow into larger bodies of water

**wetlands** Marshes, swamps, or other areas of land where the soil near the surface is soaked or covered with water

# FIND OUT MORE

## BOOKS

Bowden, Rob. *The Yangtze*. Hodder Wayland, 2005.

Leavitt, Amie Jane. *Threat to the Yangtze River Dolphin*. Mitchell Lane Publishers, 2009.

Olson, Nathan. *The Yangtze River*. Capstone Press, 2006.

Johnson, Robin and Bobbie Kalman. *Spotlight on China*. Crabtree Publishing Company, 2008

Kalman, Bobbie. *China the Land (Revised edition)*. Crabtree Publishing Company, 2008.

## WEB SITES

**ChinaCulture.org: Yangtze River**
www.culturalink.gov.cn/gb/en_travel/2003-09/24/content_34069.htm

**International Rivers: Three Gorges Dam**
www.internationalrivers.org/en/china/three-gorges-dam

**The Nature Conservancy: The Yangtze**
www.nature.org/wherewework/greatrivers/projects

**NOAA Fisheries, Office of Protected Resources: Yangtze River Dolphin**
www.nmfs.noaa.gov/pr/species/mammals/cetaceans/chineseriverdolphin.htm

**The Water Page: Yangtze River**
www.africanwater.org/yangtze.htm

## ABOUT THE AUTHOR

Molly Aloian has written more than 50 nonfiction books for children on a wide variety of topics, including endangered animals, animal life cycles, continents and their geography, holidays around the world, and chemistry. When she is not busy writing, she enjoys traveling, hiking, and cooking.

# INDEX

Page references in **bold** type are to illustrations.